CONCRETE MIXERS

by Marlene Targ Brill

PULL AHEAD BOOKS
Mighty Movers

⌞ Lerner Publications Company • Minneapolis

For this book, the author talked with many people who knew about concrete and trucks. She would like to thank Lucy Klocksin; Ann Howard; and Albert Draves, who came up with the idea of putting mixers together with trucks. Dick Carione sent the history of Draves's Chain Belt company. And Dale Stempel explained how concrete is made inside trucks. Their stories turned into this book.

Text copyright © 2007 by Marlene Targ Brill

Lerner Publications Company
A division of Lerner Publishing Group
241 First Avenue North
Minneapolis, MN 55401 U.S.A.

Website address: www.lernerbooks.com

Words in **bold** type are explained in a glossary on page 30.

Library of Congress Cataloging-in-Publication Data

Brill, Marlene Targ.
        Concrete mixers / by Marlene Targ Brill.
            p.   cm. – (Pull ahead books)
        Includes index.
        ISBN-13: 978-0-8225-6011-1 (lib. bdg. : alk. paper)
        ISBN-10: 0-8225-6011-9 (lib. bdg. : alk. paper)
        1. Concrete mixers—Juvenile literature. I. Title. II. Series.
TA439.B68 2007
624.1'834–dc22   2005017967

Manufactured in the United States of America
1 2 3 4 5 6 – JR – 12 11 10 09 08 07

Wow! What kind of truck is this?

This truck is a **concrete** mixer. But what is concrete?

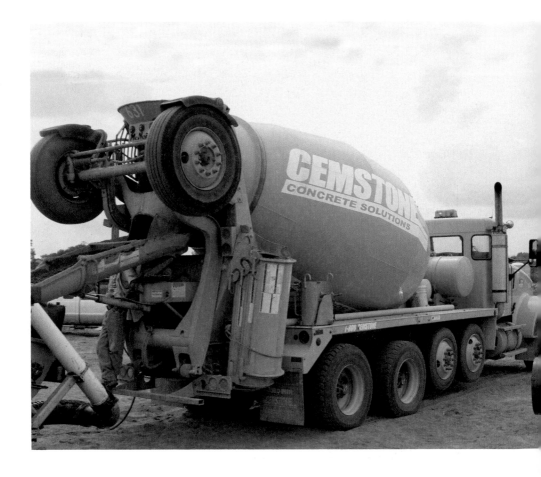

Concrete starts out as a wet, lumpy mix.

The mix is made of **cement**, a gray dust that makes concrete hard. It is also made of **gravel**, sand, and water.

When concrete dries, it is rock hard. People use concrete to make many things. Sidewalks are made of concrete.

Some buildings are made of concrete.

Many roads, bridges, and dams are made of concrete. How do concrete mixers help to make them?

Concrete mixers mix concrete. They carry concrete to where it is needed. How does the truck do these jobs?

A driver takes the truck to a concrete factory.

Click! Ping! Swish! The cement, gravel, sand, and water shoot down a big slide. The slide is called a **hopper.**

The hopper reaches into the **barrel** of the truck. The inside of the barrel is called a **drum.**

The driver climbs a ladder on the side of the truck. He looks into the hopper to make sure the drum is full.

Then the driver gets back in the **cab.** What does the driver do next?

The driver turns on the engine. Whirr!
The giant mixing machine starts to run.

16

The big barrel holding the drum turns around and around.

Fins inside the drum move in circles. The fins act like large arms. They mix the cement, gravel, sand, and water together.

Then the concrete mixer is ready to go.
Vr-rr-room! The truck rolls forward.

The giant barrel keeps spinning as the truck moves. The concrete will be ready when the truck gets to the job.

The driver parks the truck near the job.
A worker pushes a button. The button
is on the outside of the truck.

Screech! A trap door on the **chute** opens. Thick concrete slides down the chute. Workers shovel the concrete across roads or sidewalks.

They can also place it into **molds** of wood or steel. They pat it hard to squash out air bubbles.

The concrete dries in the shape of the mold.

Workers remove the mold. The concrete has hardened. What happens to the truck?

The truck is out of concrete. A worker washes the empty truck.

Then the truck goes back to the factory.
It gets more cement, gravel, sand, and
water. What will the concrete mixer
help build next?

Facts about Concrete Mixers

■ Around 1900, the first concrete mixers were iron drums that were turned by hand. Each drum sat on an iron frame. The frame was pulled by a team of horses.

■ By 1920, cars pulled mixers. The car and the mixer each had a different motor.

■ In the 1930s, the mixer and car became one truck with one motor.

■ Fins inside the drum need to go around 70 times to mix concrete.

■ The drum holds 32,000 pounds of concrete. That is enough to make a sidewalk that is 130 feet long, 5 feet wide, and 4 inches thick. This is the length of about five elephants standing end to end in a row.

Parts of a Cement Mixer

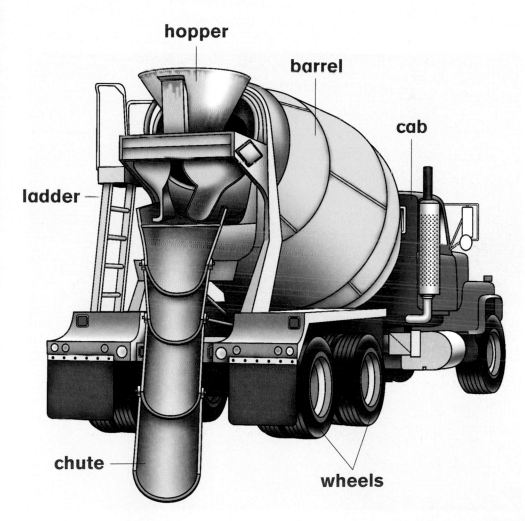

hopper

barrel

cab

ladder

chute

wheels

Glossary

barrel: the large round outside part of the drum

cab: the part of the truck where the driver sits

cement: a gray dust that makes concrete hard

chute: a slide that carries the concrete from the drum to the wheelbarrow or the ground

concrete: a mix of cement, gravel, sand, and water that becomes hard when it dries

drum: the part of the truck where concrete is mixed

fins: large arms that mix the concrete inside the drum

gravel: small stones used to make concrete

hopper: a slide that shoots cement into the drum of a truck

molds: hollow containers that are made in a particular shape. When concrete is poured into a container, it hardens in that shape.

More about Concrete Mixers

Check out these books and this website to find out more about concrete mixers.

Books

Eick, Jean. *Concrete Mixers*. Eden Prairie, MN: Child's World, 1999.
This book shows what it is like to ride inside a concrete mixer.

Katz, Bobbi. *Truck Talk: Rhymes on Wheels*. New York: Scholastic, 1997.
This book talks about many kinds of trucks in rhyme.

Simon, Seymour. *Seymour Simon's Book of Trucks*. New York: HarperCollins, 2000.
This book tells how different trucks are alike.

Website

History for Kids: Ancient Concrete
http://www.historyforkids.org/learn/architecture/concrete.htm
This site shows how early people used concrete.

Index

Photo Acknowledgments

The photographs in this book appear courtesy of: © Todd Strand/Independent Picture Service, pp. 3, 4, 10, 19, 23, 25; © Sam Lund/Independent Picture Service, pp. 5, 15, 17, 20, 21, 24, 26; Portland Cement Association, pp. 6, 13, 14; © Royalty-Free/CORBIS, p. 7; PhotoDisc Royalty Free by Getty Images, p. 9; © H. Lange/zefa/CORBIS, p. 8; © Derek M. Allan; Travel Ink/CORBIS, p. 11; © Joseph Sohm; ChromoSohm Inc./COR-BIS, p. 12; © Ernest Feland, Bobcat Company, pp. 16, 18; © Gary Moon, p. 22; © ANNEBICQUE BERNARD/CORBIS SYGMA, p. 27.

Front Cover: Photo courtesy of Mack Trucks, Inc.